P9-DGY-412

# Each Orange Had 8 Slices

## A Counting Book

by **Paul Giganti, Jr.**

pictures by **Donald Crews**

Greenwillow Books, *An Imprint of* HarperCollins*Publishers*

24
RAPIDES PARISH LIBRARY
ALEXANDRIA, LOUISIANA

WITHDRAWN FROM
RAPIDES PARISH LIBRARY

**For my wife, Judy, whose support has multiplied my efforts**
**—P. G., Jr.**

For
**—D. C.**

Gouache paints were used for the full-color art. The text type is Helvetica.

Each Orange Had 8 Slices: A Counting Book. Text copyright © 1992 by Paul Giganti, Jr. Illustrations copyright © 1992 by Donald Crews. All rights reserved. Manufactured in China. For information address HarperCollins Children's Books, a division of HarperCollins Publishers, 10 East 53rd Street, New York, NY 10022. www.harperchildrens.com First Edition 11 12 13 SCP 20 19 18 17 16 15

Library of Congress Cataloging-in-Publication Data

Giganti, Paul.
Each orange had eight slices: a counting book / by Paul Giganti, Jr.; pictures by Donald Crews.
p. cm.
"Greenwillow Books."
Summary: An illustrated introduction to counting and simple addition.
ISBN 0-688-10428-2
ISBN 0-688-10429-0 (lib. bdg.)
ISBN 0-688-13985-X (paper)
1. Counting—Juvenile literature.
[1. Counting. 2. Addition.]
I. Crews, Donald, ill.
II. Title. III. Title:
Each orange had 8 slices.
QA113.G54 1992
513.5'5—dc20 [E]
90-24167 CIP AC

On my way to the playground I saw **3** red flowers. Each red flower had **6** pretty petals. Each petal had **2** tiny black bugs.

How many red flowers were there? How many pretty petals were there? How many tiny black bugs were there in all?

On my way to school I saw
**3** little kids.
Each kid rode a tricycle.
Each tricycle had **3** wheels.

How many little kids were there?

How many tricycles were there?

How many wheels were there in all?

QUACK
QUACK
QUACK

QUACK
QUACK
QUACK

QUACK
QUACK
QUACK

QUACK
QUACK
QUACK
QUACK

QUACK
QUACK
QUACK
QUACK

QUACK
QUACK
QUACK
QUACK

QUACK
QUACK
QUACK

On my way to the zoo
I saw **3** waddling ducks.
Each duck had **4** baby ducks
trailing behind.
Each duck said,
"QUACK, QUACK, QUACK."

QUACK
QUACK
QUACK

QUACK
QUACK
QUACK

QUACK
QUACK
QUACK

QUACK
QUACK
QUACK

QUACK
QUACK
QUACK

QUACK
QUACK
QUACK

QUACK
QUACK
QUACK

How many waddling ducks were there?
How many baby ducks were there?
How many "QUACKS" were there in all?

On my way to Grandma's
I saw **2** fat cows.
Each cow had **2** calves.
Each calf had **4** skinny legs.

How many fat cows were there?
How many calves were there?
How many legs were there in all?

On my way to the circus
I saw **2** colorful clowns.
Each clown was holding
**1** bunch of balloons
in each hand. Each bunch
had **5** bright balloons.

How many colorful
clowns were there?
How many bunches
of balloons were there?
How many bright balloons
were there in all?

On my way to the freeway
I saw **4** huge trucks.
Each truck had **2** long trailers.
Each trailer had **4** giant letters
that spelled ACME.

How many huge trucks were there?
How many long trailers were there?
How many giant letters
were there in all?

On my way to lunch I ate
**2** juicy oranges. Each orange had **8** slices.
Each slice had **2** small seeds.

How many juicy oranges were there?

How many slices were there?

How many seeds were there in all?

On my way to the store I saw **4** trees.
Each tree had **3** bird's nests.
Each bird's nest had **2** spotted eggs.

How many trees were there?

How many bird's nests were there?

How many spotted eggs
were there in all?

On my way to my friend's house
I bought **3** bags of gum balls.
Each bag had **3** small boxes inside.
Each box contained **6** gum balls.

How many bags of gum balls were there?
How many small boxes were there?
How many gum balls were there in all?

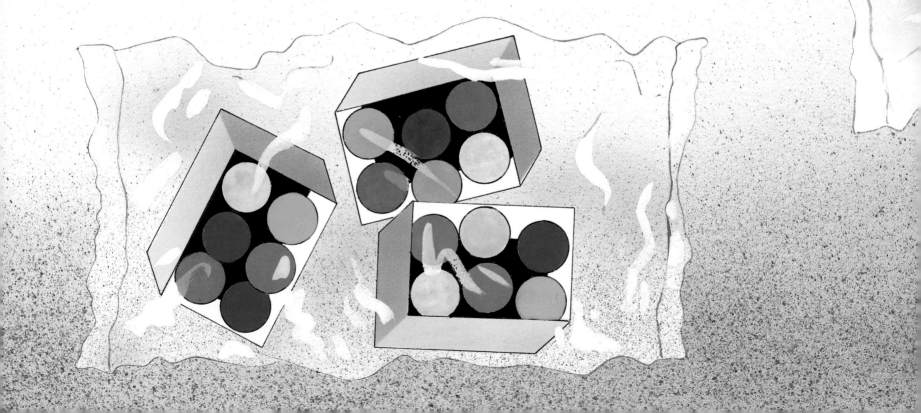

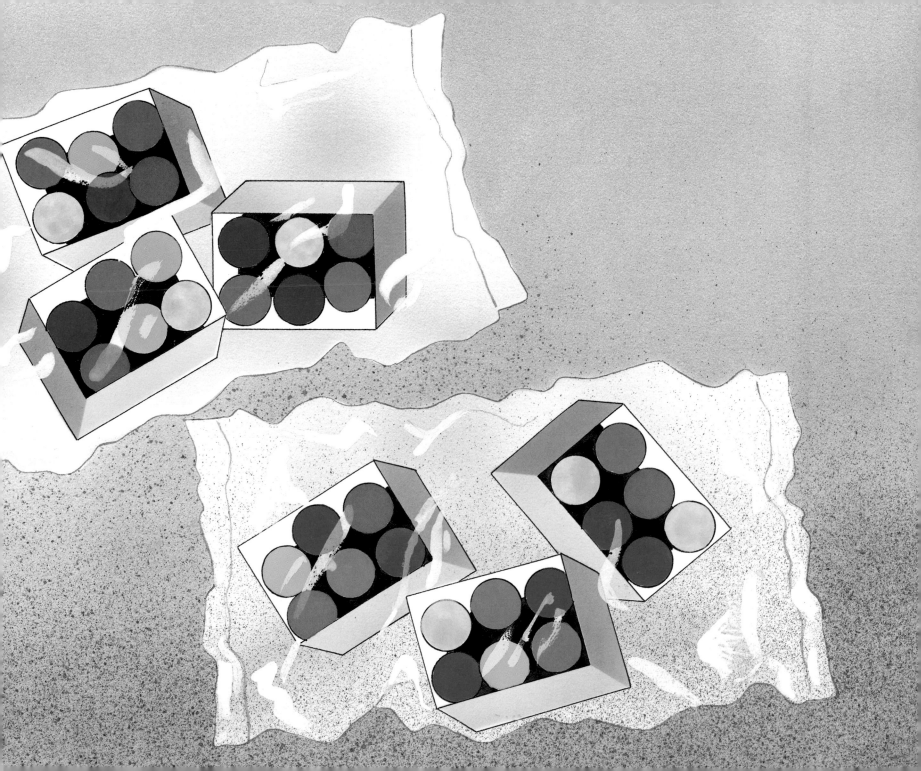

On my way home I passed
**3** yellow houses.
Each yellow house had
**3** red flower pots.
Each flower pot
had **5** blue flowers.

How many yellow houses
were there?
How many red flower pots
were there?
How many blue flowers
were there in all?

Before my bedtime
I read **2** books.
Each book had
**10** big pages.
Each page had
**1** pretty picture.

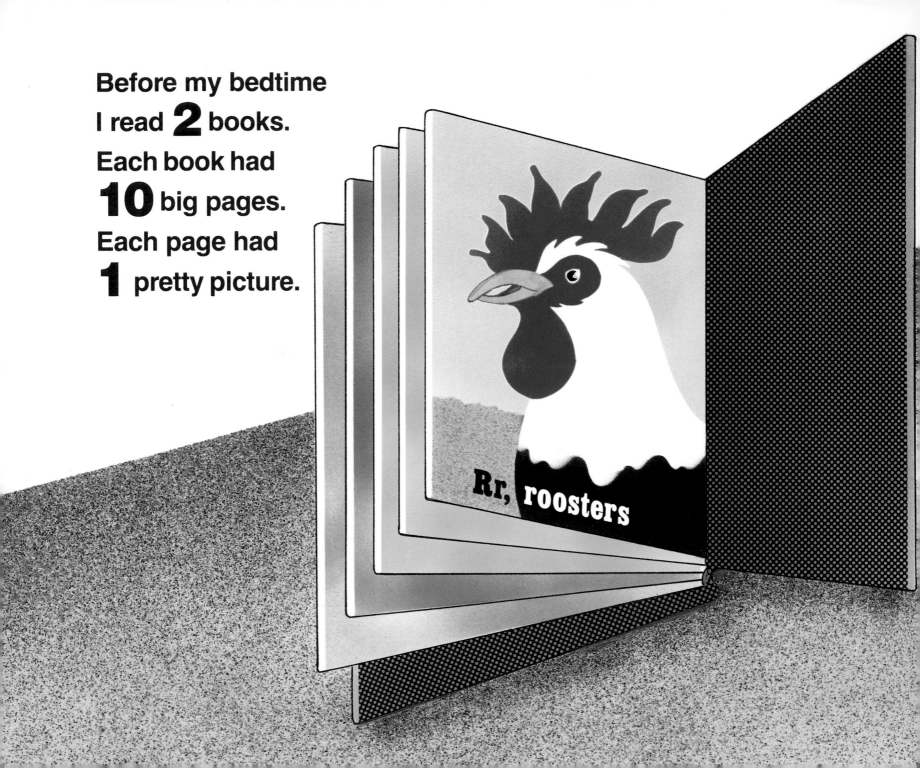

Rr, roosters

How many books were there?
How many big pages were there?
How many pretty pictures were there in all?

Ss, sunsets

On the last page of the last book,
I found this poem:

"As I was going to St. Ives,
I met a man with 7 wives.
Every wife had 7 sacks.
Every sack had 7 cats.
Every cat had 7 kittens.
Kittens, cats, sacks,
and wives,
How many were going
to St. Ives?"

Answer: Just 1 person—me.